THE CRAZY BUNCH

THE CRAZY BUNCH

WILLIE PERDOMO

PENGUIN POETS

PENGUIN BOOKS
An imprint of Penguin Random House LLC
penguinrandomhouse.com

LIBRARY OF CONGRESS CATALOGING-IN-PUBLICATION DATA
Names: Perdomo, Willie, author.
Title: The crazy bunch / Willie Perdomo.
Description: [New York] : Penguin Books, an imprint of Penguin Random House
    LLC, [2019] | Series: Penguin poets |
Identifiers: LCCN 2018047501 (print) | LCCN 2018049478 (ebook) | ISBN
    9780525504627 () | ISBN 9780143132691
Classification: LCC PS3566.E691216 (ebook) | LCC PS3566.E691216 A6 2019
    (print) | DDC 811/.54—dc23
LC record available at https://lccn.loc.gov/2018047501

Printed in the United States of America
10 9 8 7 6 5 4 3 2 1

Set in Sabon LT Std
Designed by Elyse J. Strongin, Neuwirth & Associates

for NERUDA PERDOMO

CONTENTS

". . . to be our own, to be electric, fresh . . ."

—Walt Whitman

THE POETRY COPS
(Consolidated Poetry Systems)

COPS: That's you and who else in this picture?

PAPO: That's me, Phat Phil, Nestor, Petey, Dre, and Angel. That was a Friday night. We were lamping in front of 2026 Lexington Avenue, near Gaddafi's all-night spin counter. The Bruja on the second floor was arranging a *preparación* for us. You could call it a freedom party.

COPS: Preparations? You mean reparations?

PAPO: You know, like protection, spirit guides, *caminos*, higher powers, pigeon-chasing.

COPS: Twenty twenty-six. That's where you found—

PAPO: Yellow tops, back-to-life summers, "9½," first kisses, cop chases, catch-n-kill for real. Twenty twenty-six was the beginning, the end, lingua franca, the hill & bottom.

COPS: They called you Skinicky. Is that right?

PAPO: They still call me Skinicky.

COPS: Bagging up bricks and writing poems Skinicky?

PAPO: I wrote more bricks than poems; bagged up, all together, less than a brick but came out with at least half a book.

COPS: But it's true you *were* writing poems.

PAPO: Bro, poems were falling from the rooftops, flailing out the windows; sometimes you'd pick up the corner pay phone and a poem would be calling collect.

COPS: Can we talk about Josephine?

PAPO: Beginnings should come with a starter kit. Sometimes I feel like I dreamed Josephine. Like for real.

COPS: We thought we could help you remember.

PAPO: Man, had to be at least five presidents and a breakfast since I've seen Josephine.

COPS: You were the first one, she said. To find Nestor.

PAPO: She didn't say that. Angel was the first one to find Nestor. But I was there when Dre decided he wanted to be an archangel. Every age requires a new lens, at least one pair of dress pants, and a dope whatever you need to witness. I'm saying, we gave Grandmaster Flash & the Furious Five their controlling symbol.

COPS: How so?

PAPO: You know, broken glass everywhere. Street games before the rules changed. We'd line up empty pints, fifths & quarts on a plank, walk twenty paces to a five-gallon bucket brimmed with small chunks of Manhattan schist, and we would commence to slinging them shits; testing our angry range, our winning-shot fantasies, developing a penchant for target & aim, beauty & blame.

COPS: How long were you down with the Crazy Bunch?

PAPO: I'm still down with the Crazy Bunch.

COPS: Let's start with the Bruja on that Friday night.

PAPO: For some of us, telling a story, or hearing one on the humble, meant clearing a path, booking a cruise to self-knowledge, and for others it meant getting some ass. No passive thinking. You couldn't be caught blinking when you told a story. Question is, who's left for the telling and who tells about the leaving after they been left.

COPS: So, who's left?

PAPO: What set us off is the same thing that set us apart, you could say. That weekend our endings were paid in full. No matter where we went, the search for a loving eye was in effect. But there's some shit I promised to take to the grave. Y'all know how that go.

Tell me the story
Of all these things.
Beginning wherever you wish, tell even us.

—Theresa Hak Kyung Cha, *Dictee*

"Tell it. Tell it for real."

—Brother Lo

IN THE FACE OF WHAT YOU REMEMBER

In the Face of What You Remember

You remember, that was the summer of Up Rock, quarter water,
    speed knots, pillow bags, two-for-five, Jesus pieces, and
    Bambú. The Willie Bobo was turned up to ten, and some
    would've said that a science was dropped on our summer.

The summer that was lit with whispers of wild style, Rock
    Steady battles & white party plates made all kinds of
    moons on the playground foam.

The summer the Burner was used to eat & mandate, inspired
    Sunday sermons, became a literary influence with humming
    climaxes, a bribable tale, a dub tied to a string &
    squashing beef wasn't an option.

The summer of fresh shrills, and a future somersaulting off a
    monkey bar; a future placing bets that all us old heads,
    desperate to find a new cool, could not flip pure.

That was the summer that our grills dropped to below freezing.

Back then, Palo Viejo was thermal & therapy, bones were
    smoked in the cut, and you had to expect jungle gym giggle
    to be accompanied by buckshot.

That was the summer Charlie Chase hijacked megawatts from
    Rosa's kitchenette, found gems in a milk crate, spun his one
    & twos below rims that still vibrated with undocumented
    double-dunks.

The same summer we became pundits & philosophers, poets
    & pushers; that we all tried to fly, but only one of us
    succeeded.

The summer that Papu turned up to extra status. The only one in
    the crew who had reduced fame's window by a fifth when
    the camera panned his Cazal-laced Up Rock in the Roxy
    scene of *Beat Street*.

One could say we gave the Block gasp & gossip, body & bag,
   a folktale worth its morphology.

That was the season we had reason to rock capes & wings,
   chains & rings, some of us flew Higher than most, and
   tricks were hardly ever pulled from a hat; all that, & a bag
   of BBQ Bon Tons was enough for at least one of us to say,

I'm straight.

Bad Habits

Petey liked to twist the right end of his mustache when he was
    listening for updates. (Y'all remember Petey. He was always
    on that chuck chill-out tip, but most days he didn't get
    to choose.)

When he ignited a squabble, Chuna would slap his right thigh to
    get every syllable out with a violent scansion.

Tommy Lee threw rocks at unsuspecting pigeons.

Dwight kept his right hand tucked into the crotch of his Lees,
    steady stunting on some *bollo*.

Angel bit his tongue when he wanted to ask a question.

Max counted his money and his money counted him.

Brother Lo liked to whistle "All the Things You Are" when it
    rained that Puerto Rico rain.

Chee-Wa's nose used to break out into an anxious table of
    contents when he was skied up.

Papu would dance if he wanted to make a point. So, imagine
    him saying, *Nah, nah, nah, fuck that shit*, and poppin' &
    lockin' on every word.

Nestor hated the words *Stop, I was only playing*.

Loco Tommy blinked three times, convulsively, and then tapped
    the right side of his face against his right shoulder blade.

Jujo spit and spit and spit and spit.

Popeye had a villainous laugh.

Dre loved to crash revivals.

Chino Chan did back handsprings from sewer to sewer
   whenever he received good news.

Georgie could scratch his ankle straight through a
   graveyard shift.

The first thing out of Skinicky's mouth was always a feeling.

The Day of Our Founding

Dwight was going to the D, the mighty
D, where Rosie, Sonia, Debbie, Cachita,
Shameka, her sisters, and Josephine's
cousin from Wagner liked to castle &
smoke, swear & secret, share hoops &
slap their Bostons on the chess tables.

Slick Vic, Tyrone, Junebug & Heck Collect
had set up a Florsheim *guiso*. There were
two plans to crash Josephine's Sweet 16.
Nestor, Dre, and Petey got freshly dipped,
& went to the Deuce to catch & take flicks.

Almost twenty-five deep chillin' on two
masticated benches, and Nestor said:

    TCB. The Crazy Bunch.

By that age, Nestor had groomed a full
beard, rocked all kinds of captain, 52'd
his way through an apache line of Down
Brothers, & we were all there when he
flipped a half-pike off five cake-stacked
mattresses that shimmied with blackouts.

Naturally. (You have to recall, that day
was puffed & passed, and Skinicky said,

    Naturally.

Purple City hollered, *You heard this
nigga? This nigga just said, "Naturally."*)

The spliff was choo-choo'd, the guffaw
lit—shit, you laughed too, so naturally
Dre, who had a boom decisive left hook,

only two words to say at a party minus
two steps at a jam, who was the only
one to draw one-on-one with Nestor,
nodded his head, cosigned, and said:

Word. The Crazy Bunch.

Head Crack Head Crack

Zoo Bang
Auld Lang

Brick City
Fly Ditty

Drug War
Street Noir

War Fat
Bank That

Sneaker Box
Check Account

Get Fresh
Stay Fly

Night Pool
Old School

Stash House
Corner Store

We Cool
No More

Smoked Out
Player's Ball

Okey Doke
Flat Broke

Hang Out
No Doubt

Black Out
Death Count

Dwight Gone
Tone Gone

Petey Gone
Chino Gone

Body Shot
Chop Shop

Black Hole
Myths Sold

Break That
Like This

Black Cat
Death Kiss

Power Move
Move That

Krush Groove
Dope Shit

Step Back
Get This

THE POETRY COPS

PAPO: That's Nestor at the *preparación*. He didn't like messing with saints & songs, and shit. But he went anyway, on the strength.

COPS: What's wrong with his eyes?

PAPO: Nothing, he's just in his truth.

COPS: Did anyone else get prepared that night?

PAPO: All of us. One by one. Starting with Angel. The Bruja told Nestor she saw something, but Nestor said, *Don't tell me. I don't want to know.* Better to unknow and find yourself in the knowing, you know what I'm saying? But look carefully at the Bruja. Look at the background. How many hands you see?

COPS: That looks like a blur in the exposure to me.

PAPO: You could call it a "blur," but that same hand might be touching you right now.

COPS: Could be the raindrops on the window too.

PAPO: All I know is that I stomp the floor three times with my right foot whenever I take a shower.

COPS: Who was under the bedsheet?

PAPO: That was me. By that point, I had already left the living room. My heartbeat was big that night. Cold Crush big. You could fit thimbles in my nostrils. I still have a piece of the coconut that I threw off the rooftop.

COPS: C'mon, stop with that chicken blood voodoo.

PAPO: I'm just saying, man, the Bruja wore white for a whole year. Can't fool with someone who wears white for a whole year. Let's say you see a trail of cigar smoke streaming down Lexington Avenue—you know where there's smoke there must be a past. I don't really believe in ghosts like that, but, yo, if you stand on the corner long enough there's some shit that you can see coming.

Some Things You Might Need to Start Your Day

An egg yolk
A dollop of white sugar
A broken scissor blade
Double palm strips
Coconut oil
A stick of yage
Pull the shades up
A fat Buddha
Two dream crystals
Some dirt from Utuado
A peculiar heart
An old movie ticket
Yellow *collares*
A crown of bananas
Red *collares*
A mini notebook
Green *collares*
A tiny pencil
White *collares*
A miniature glass clown
Two fish bones
A love letter from Rikers
Four white candles
A cut ribbon
An old photo
Your baby shoes
A pineapple
A bowl of seedless grapes
One tangerine
A *puro*
A bowl of daisies
Clap three times &
Let the work
Do its job

We Used to Call It Puerto Rico Rain

The rain had just finished saying, *This block is mine.*

The kind of rain where you could sleep through two
> breakthroughs, and still have enough left to belly-sing
> the ambrosial hour.

Blood pellets in the dusk & dashes of hail were perfect for
> finding new stashes; that is to say, visitations were never
> announced.

A broken umbrella handle posed a question by the day
> care center.

A good time to crush a love on a stoop, to narrate through
> a window, to find the heartbeat of solitude, and collect
> gallons for the Bruja's next *baño*.

Good conditions to be in the dialectic of O Wow Ooo Baby O
> Shit Ooo Damn.

The perfect weather to master the art of standing under a bodega
> awning, shifting crisis to profit.

There's always a dreamer who thinks they can race the rain to
> the building, who loves the smell of wet concrete, and uses
> a good downpour to be discreet.

There's always one toddler who quietly crawls off the top step,
> dodges a thunderbolt, and quickly becomes fluent in all
> things stormy weather.

Story goes that Don Julio was swept up, ripped around the
> corner, stumbled & cartwheeled to the light post, but he
> never let go of his porkpie hat.

An improvised ballet near an improvised rivulet.

Shopping bags, pulverized by branches, contort into a new
     nation of black flags. Our block was our island.

The manhole on the corner perked with popsicle sticks, empty
     beer cans, and the brown sole of a fake karate slipper as we
     started to sink & boil.

The forecast, you said, *was type perfect.*

At the Preparación

Mothers will always ask about the state of your tranquillity.

Every block had a *cemi*. Someone who wasn't afraid of being
     taken from the present. Her name was usually Cuca.

To get to the *preparación* you have to go on a mission. Nothing
     impossible, but nothing that you could repeat.

When you get to the palm tree on the corner, back up and take a
     left. You know there are no palm trees in the street, so you
     take a right.

A mute Siamese cat will dare you with a quick scurry into
     Gaddafi's.
Go left, again, but just a *chín*.
Go right, again, but just a *chín*.

Turn slow at the third corner, as if you were an uptown eclipse,
     an indecisive twilight, a fix ready to burn.

When you feel a follicle of sweat grovel down your back, you
     have arrived.

You will see an altar in the living room.
The altar should be stacked with some
things you might need to start your day.

Tato Brujo will have his back toward you.
Make sure that he's facing San Lazaro.
Make sure his chants trumpet the rain's insistence.

When the *preparación* begins, they will pencil your wish on a
     slip of brown paper bag, and one by one they will dip your
     real name in a mug of honey.

You tell the Bruja, *I could use a blessing.* She pushes up and says,
*I walked a long way, left dust tracks on the road, all the
poems you wrote are stories I done told.*

You've seen that moment: a clap, an instant, a jab, a pair of
hands soaked in rubbing alcohol, a flame, a vicious blue.

The fire you can make.
The light, not so much.

You swear that you can see through walls.
As much as you know, you can't know.

Yo, Nestor says, *tell her to leave me alone, man.*

Campeche's painting of Jesús Cristo looks at Petey with a
sketch eye.

Throw this coconut over your shoulder, the Bruja will say. *Make
sure you throw it high, so it splatters into a million little
pieces, and tell me which piece is looking back at you.*

Juice & Butter

That was the summer we rolled deep in the pursuit of
    Juice & Butter.

Juice was a wink underwater,
a finger snap in a dark hallway,
a backward salute across one
neckline, a club of coded fists.

Butter was weigh money, out-of-
town connects, leather bombers,
Virgin Mary medallions, Starfire
rubies, a suite full of wet labia.

The stink talk
The legit blue

The last outlaw
The uncut raw

The right true
The bright cue

Bundles & stacks
Brims & kicks

The fresh racks
The new blacks

The fly shit
The clean hit

Juice

Could cut the line
Could skip the line
Could draw the line
Could book you before
You got booked.

Simple. Front and discover that there's no future in fronting.

Fronting: like acting bigger than your true size, like having
    pretensions, like you ain't really

> *Nothing/nothing*
> *nothing/nothing.*

Like saying you know when you don't.
Like knowing, and still saying you don't.
Like saying you won't, but you do.
Like swearing you didn't, but you did.

   Juice.

Juice met you going up the stairs &
left you swinging out the window.

   Butter.

Butter recouped what remained from a
guiso, and opened up the next morning.

Juice threw two fingers up from three blocks away, chopped
    them off an avenue later & posted them first class the
    next day.

Juice delivered, ordered, stamped & bagged.

If you started a story,

Juice was there to finish it.

Dapper Dan Meets Petey Shooting Cee-Lo

The forecast called for the rawness, a litany of daps & pounds,
    denim two-pieces, bucket hats, and velour tracksuits.

This is before the world went 2.0.

You used the word *money* like
Pretty Tony *I got money, I got money*
Or Tony Rome *I want my money*
Or Kizack Wizack *What's good, money?*
Or like Rehab Roger, who upon dishing a concept would say,
I'm giving you good money, man.

Having just finished shooting trips, Petey gripped a palmful of
    Grants & Benjamins, and his pupils were dilated to
    the riches.

Street games fade one dream into another: You bet on your best
    hope, and what you gonna do with all that scrilla fluttering
    in the oval.

Angel sorted his ducats, kept the faces on his bills skyward.
Phat Phil's inside pocket was packed with penny candies.

You always knew there was a price for head cracks.

A legion of Old-Schoolers flanked the bank: Black Rob,
    Hollywood from *A Bunch of Grapes*, Krip & Spy, Kong &
    Papo Kong, steady flashing knots, still opening spots.

By that time, Hollywood's total net in dirty money had reached
    short of a million were it not for the million and one shorts
    he took.

You had to be laced to loot.
The clack of die, shoot.
You stir-fry nigga, shoot.
Hollywood said, *I would if I could.*

Dapper Dan was just walking down Lexington, on his way to his
shop on 125th Street, a fresh LV stitched into his Stacy's, a
clutch to match, and asked *Who got the bank* on a whim
because the day always comes when you have to put the
past up for grabs; where, really, you learn that sometimes
you get dressed up just to lose.

Guiso at Florsheim's

All you had to say was *I'm down.*

A box of black Hefty bags.
Wire cutters & a crowbar.
Two ropes & a dirty rag.
One bike, a getaway car.

A collage of curious faces.
A class in paying attention.
The history of false starts.
A displaced apprehension.

Whistle twice if Teddy-Up stalls.
Whistle thrice on a backup call.

Wire. Cut. Step.
Repeat.
Wire. Shit. Step.
Repeat.
Wire. What. Step.
Repeat.
Wire. But. Wait.
Repeat.
Wire. Oh. Shit.
Repeat.

A double-headed light exposes the cracks in the planks, an
        assembly line of breaking & entering, rats hurry back into
        their holes, a spiderweb as big as a building—click, the
        alarm rings the song of the shank through barbed wire.

Cut out, oh shit, let's dip.
Cut out, oh shit, boom bip.
Cut out, oh shit, these don't fit.
Cut out, oh shit, size five or six?

Hefty bags bombed from the rooftop like parachutes filled with
British Walkers, Clydes, Chuck Taylors & suede Ballys.

A reception squad waited at the bottom, and just like that a new
shorty becomes down with the vanguard.

A rumble down a fire escape, screen action hero jumps off a
ledge, synchronized landings, no soundtrack, and if you
asked us, that night we learned to find our way in the dark.

THE POETRY COPS

PAPO: Check out my blue suede Clydes.

COPS: Is that a Chi Modu photo?

PAPO: Check out those fat laces. That was *guiso* booty.

COPS: I love the symmetry in your poses.

PAPO: Funky funky fresh with the funky style.

COPS: That looks like the old triple X Times Square.

PAPO: Yeah, man, all kinds of deep throats, but that's the Deuce of 7 *Grandmasters, 5 Fingers of Death, The 36th Chamber of Shaolin.*

COPS: That sounds like the beginning of a poem.

PAPO: We only saw like a third of the flicks that night.

COPS: Maybe if we talk about the Dreads.

PAPO: When you left your apartment today, after your coffee with two sugars, after your morning paper, did you think, *Shit, this is it, this might be the day I check out of the Friendly Motor Inn.*

COPS: Okay, so, let's get back to what you and the rest of the crew found when you returned from Times Square.

PAPO: I can't tell you what happened to Nestor. Even if I knew, I couldn't tell you.

COPS: Well, why not just tell us what you saw.

PAPO: Sometimes that phantom has a way of pulling up in front of the building like one preview too many.

Triple Feature

Triple feature at the Deuce, extra-butter popcorn, a grip of loose
    joints & a quart of Olde English 800 to chase the Snoopies.

The trip was just starting to seek real estate and the glee in our
    marquee was sold out.

Time to find your Drunken Monkey style with Brass
    Monkey swigs.

Express to Grand Central, electric boogie past that old hot dog
    stand, past the new-release Fania records, past the diva's
    neon wigs—better rock your Lees right, boy.

Novelty nunchakus, the grip of tar & bubble gum on your
    sneaker sole & the right script for the right role.

The dazzle of the erotic.
The quest for the hypnotic.
The Doo-Wop bombastic.

First, flicks.
Then, flicks.

On the way back to the Block we booked free rides on the
    Shaolin Shuttle.

Lip-synced sound effects, hopped off two-seaters, snaked around
    poles, swung from straphanger to straphanger,

> *You have offended our block* (lip-sync),
> *and it's time* (lip-sync)
> *to get* (lip-sync) *fucked up.*

Petey laughed fun-house hard, and popcorn trickled from
    his lips.
Skinicky was in between cars, crying & laughing at the
    same time.

Petey, Nestor said, *your teeth are falling out of your mouth, bro.*

When you're trapped in the middle of a divine comedy, sporting
permanent creases, there's no one to show you the way out.

Angel said, *Yo, I feel like this train is falling, but it's falling up.*

Nestor said, *Stop. Please. This is a dream, right?*

Then we laughed harder, and every *blanco* looked like a death
wish logged into a diary.

C'mon, man, stop playing, Nestor said.

Later, the Block heard that Nestor ran all the way to East
Harlem, nonstop, humming Lisa Lisa's "I Wonder If I Take
You Home."

There's a flick from that night: a crew of us rocking name
buckles with styles that couldn't catch up to our faces.

SUCKER FOR LOVE ASS NIGGA

THE POETRY COPS TALK WITH PHAT PHIL

PHAT PHIL: This one? This one is at Josephine's Sweet 16. The party was at El Maestro on Southern Boulevard. We didn't rock with the BX like that, but we went on the strength.

COPS: Skinicky says he fell in love with Josephine at the party. Is that accurate?

PHAT PHIL: He was in love with her way before that. He just didn't know it. Sucker for love ass nigga.

COPS: No one wants to talk about Nestor.

PHAT PHIL: What's there to talk about?

COPS: There has to be closure, no? There has to be a resolution.

PHAT PHIL: All I know is that Nestor ran all the way to 123rd from the Deuce. All the way. Without stopping. Put that in your notebook.

COPS: How do you know, Phil?

PHAT PHIL: Because he told me, nigga. And call me Phat Phil. Nestor stood lamping on the Block, and Petey was holding him down. That's what we did. We held each other down.

COPS: I guess you had interests to protect on the Block.

PHAT PHIL: C'mon, man, stop with the Willie Bobo. I saw Nestor and I saw Petey before I got on the train to go to Josephine's party. That Snoopy they dropped had them twenty thousand leagues under the city with the woo woo woo.

COPS: Let's talk about Josephine & Skinicky, then.

PHAT PHIL: Cool, because that's where I was. I was at the party. I was trying to get with Nena, who is now my wife. You can ask her. I was at the party all night.

COPS: What do you remember about the party?

PHAT PHIL: Not for nothing, honestly & truthfully, I remember dancing with Josephine's grandmother and Skinicky yelled, *Spin her, spin her, spin her!*

Josephine's Sweet 16

By the time we got to Josephine's Sweet 16 there were cheese
    doodle fingers everywhere.

Phat Phil was already deep into his fake *Pachanga*.
Skinicky, Angel & Dre set up a snap shop by the cake tiers.

Josephine's eyes were lit like strobes & glitter, her silver dress
    hardly fit her, & because Angel was still tripping, he saw
    sequin in everything: quinine in the ice cream, a fork &
    spoon standoff; he even saw his fate in a rack of plastic
    champagne glasses, bubbles big as balloons released into
    the sky all at once. *C'mon, bro, you can't mess with a man
    who's wearing a tuxedo,* he said.

Cubes of cheddar & *guayaba* sat like Zen masters on the spheres
    of Ritz Crackers.

Josephine's brother kept adjusting his top hat because he had to
    give away his sister. Told us to stay by the roundtable just
    in case she tried to roll out and get reborn all of a sudden.

Josephine graced her gold-plated throne. Her reinvention was
    imminent.

Put on your cake face, Angel said.

What we thought we heard Skinicky say was, *If Sekhmet created
    the desert with a breath, then Shorty Bon Bon split the
    Atlantic to death.*

Party over here, party over there, and this rite you get to take
    with you.

The grown-ups spent most of their free time in the bathroom,
    and whenever the DJ played El Gran Combo, we all sighed
    & dipped to the staircase to make out, roll up, or add up.

Little Joe, Josephine's uncle, tried to call us out on our
   stagnancy—*nondisciplined knuckleheads,* he'd say; and, as
   a way of offering evidence, he'd point to Phat Phil, & there
   was Phat Phil crashing into the VIP table. Almost made
   Josephine's *abuelita* spill her rum until *abuelita* threw him
   a lifesaving turn, and spun Phat Phil back into his sea.

There's that moment right when the flashbulb flashed on
   Josephine's smile, where your sense of lottery & random
   tries to reason with you, and, yet, there's just enough
   chance to survive more than one fresh hell and emerge
   without taking shorts.

At the Battle

There's only air & opportunity between

you & the world.

Some crews fight for corners.
Some crews fight for blood.

Some crews fight for love.
Some crews fight for rights.

Some crews fight for flags.
Some crews fight for brags.

The Old-Schoolers used to send us
back to fight, so you never ran.

Hearts had to be certified &
prepared for daily pop quizzes.

Had to be ready for that sweet
place in the sun to say,

You fuckin' with the wrong one.

Sure enough, we weren't the only crew thinking about crashing
things, & heroes were for extra-mustard hot dogs on
Sundays at the Cosmo.

Even if you were good with your dukes, you still had to Up
Rock against cats from the Boogie Down, and when they
crossed the Bridge, they always thought shit was over
before it started.

At the battle, you could detect which rhymes were bit,
which rhymes were counterfeit, which bars were
written & which top-five rhymes were freestyled.

Nothing bloody, but you could tell why we talked with
   our hands.

An ex–Savage Samurai stepped in between Papu and Freeze and
   said, *Y'all just can't stand there and look at each other.*
   Somebody has to swing.

Harlem Cowboys were still part of the air, still drawing on who's
   left to talk about the last face they saw before it all went
   down, before you left town.

The legend held that myths made the music and rush hour made
   you rich, but this was a different decade.

The cipher of testimonies were correctional legacies, a stitch to
   make a vest, and someone to regale with that day's events.

Silly rhymes were like petty crimes—nothing at stake but
   city time.

You could be rich in battle but poor in moves, so you had to flip
   medieval fast.

Play yourself, & get slayed from first to last stop.

Papu synchronized his shell-toes with a gangster head nod, spun
   revolutions with a Kangol bell at peace on his head, &
   went and turned his legs into scissors.

You knew what *freeze* meant, but you've never seen someone
   frosty freeze.

It didn't matter who was carrying, more so how long you were
   carried before someone decided to drop you.

THE POETRY COPS

COPS: This one looks like a DeCavara.

PAPO: That's Nestor in the shadow. Every time the landlord fixed the vestibule light, we would blow it out, and that shadow made customers think twice about having the wrong idea. SHAKER took that flick. He used to run with ZEPHYR and those East Side Partner cats. Nice with the lens.

COPS: Who's holding the trophy?

PAPO: That's Tommy Lee. Goya all-star MVP. Tommy Lee used to bat cross-handed until he started playing in Central Park. Seen him turn doubles into triples, and gun down Triple-A players with a sixth-grade arm.

COPS: Is that Héctor Camacho? The fighter?

PAPO: Yessir. That's the Macho Man himself. He used to come to the park jams, do his *dale huevo* rocking his gladiator helmets, war bonnets, headdresses & that dookie nameplate. Shit, that nameplate went from shoulder to shoulder for real.

COPS: The Crazy Bunch had a float at the parade?

PAPO: Something like that. We basically bum-rushed the Goya float.

COPS: Love those Afros on you guys. Must be class picture day.

PAPO: Yeah, that's some ungawa black power right there. That's *difunto* Dwight, *difunto* Chino Chan, Davi, Felix, and Little Eddie on picture day at P.S. 7. Afro angels playing the back row.

COPS: These two look very Jesse James.

PAPO: That's *difunto* Marc and Baby Los. Check those flavors, though. That was after the Florsheim *guiso*. The whole Block had on fresh kicks. Even the Bruja rocked her white Royal Lo PRO-Keds: the ones with the red & blue hash on the side.

COPS: Who was locked up in this photo?

PAPO: I never understood those palm trees in the prison pics.

COPS: And this one?

That's My Heart Right There

We used to say,
That's my heart right there.

As if to say,
Don't mess with her right there.

As if, don't even play,
That's a part of me right there.

In other words, okay okay,
That's the start of me right there.

As if, come that day,
That's the end of me right there.

As if, push come to shove,
I would fend for her right there.

As if, come what may,
I would lie for her right there.

As if, come love to pay,
I would die for that right there.

Sucker for Love Ass Nigga

I.

Skinicky
Jimbrowski ass nigga
That sucker for love ass nigga

The love that gives you a pound
The love that blooms & blushes
The love that sees you around
The love that scars & shushes

The love that cries the wrong name
The love that pulls the right trigger
The love that's true to the game
The love that says, *Fuck you, nigga*

The love you work hard to forget
The love that likes to point fingers
The love that curses & sweats
The love that plays backup singer

The love that truths when it writes
The love that days when it nights

II.

Skinicky.
Jimbrowski ass nigga.
That sucker for love ass nigga.

He liked to be sad for fun.
Every New Year's Eve he'd walk up and down 125th Street
     looking for Josephine. He would put his ear to the curb to
     listen for her footsteps; even walked into the 25th Precinct
     to see if any desk appearance tickets had been issued in
     her name.

He joined freestyle ciphers with everything he would've said,
given another chance.

Brother Lo once said, *Heartbreaks need corroborations, so you
have to commit everything to memory, no paper.*

Who had software to guarantee that none of us would crash?

III.

The rules of engagement:

Whenever you walk with your boo, make sure
she's always on your left side, inside the curb.
Tell her how you feel, but never the last word.
Platinum, gold—they're just medals.
Let her pedal the ten-speed sometimes.
She'll tell you when she wants you to know.

There was nothing that included the word *settle* in Josephine's
style.

None of us had girls, so how to say *That's my woman.*

That night, Skinicky had the nerve to pull out his black
composition book.

In all of her waking language, Josephine needed to be free. She
put her hand up like a crossing guard. *Wait up*, she said.
There you go. Already putting shit in the game.

The windows were marauded by twilight, and it was a beautiful
summer to be a sucker for love ass nigga. All you had to do
was surrender.

Skinicky tried to hit her with some Shalamar. *"It's got to be real.
Girl, I could write a book on how you're making me feel."*

Then Josephine turned her neck and rolled her eyes. *Say it right,*
she said. *Let it all be automatic true. Don't be shook. Don't*
book. Be good in this dream. According to you, she said,
I never use the right words. Can you read me now? Don't
name what it's not, but don't stand there and try to sky me.
Ain't that much poetry in the world, she said.

IV.

You could say that Josephine lived in a virtuous time. She had
a habit of cutting you short when you came up to her
and said, *I'm gonna tell you something, but you have to*
promise not to tell anyone.

She bulleted the abuses, the excuses, the short
fuses, & then she hit Skinicky with her dream:
She saw zero, so liberation was on the menu.
Mister Softee vanilla so sweet it was forbidden.
A baguette meant bounty, so we can all eat.
A beige pair of heels told her to stay neutral.
There was a seven so her mental was on point.
A glass of water rushed to leave its solutions.

Don't even try to open any thank-you notes here, she said.
Before the lonely pays a social call, stay faithful to the bad
& the wrong. Don't worry about my heart; it'll remember
what it's supposed to remember. Don't forget the first rule,
baby: Write about what you know.

Her last word was

Siempre,

& then she went silent like a blank piece of paper.

Two couplets later, Skinicky was back on the Block heading
straight toward the Age of Fuck It, and it was true then, as
it is now, that there were only a few of us holding the street
down with our hearts.

THE POETRY COPS TALK WITH JOSEPHINE

COPS: Skinicky told us you were his heart.

JOSEPHINE: Papo was lying.

COPS: We spoke to a few people from Lexington that swear by it.

JOSEPHINE: In the morning you want all the bad shit to be gone.

COPS: He said you were his beautiful battle.

JOSEPHINE: Yeah, he liked that word a lot. *Beautiful.*

COPS: He called you a *real dream.*

JOSEPHINE: You know dreams are the only time you can wake up before someone pulls a trigger.

COPS: We want to hear your side, Josephine.

JOSEPHINE: When slick shows up it makes my hands sweat and I don't do old love.

COPS: But what if it was true?

JOSEPHINE: You can't freestyle the truth and I told him, *Once you start using the word* soul, *you start wanting things you can't have.*

COPS: But what if, though?

JOSEPHINE: I dig it. Sometimes you have to fantasize to your favorite ifs. What do you keep to yourself just in case you have to run away?

COPS: We just want to help Skinicky. That's all. He's trying to remember.

JOSEPHINE: I used to ask him, *What's going to happen when the words stop working?* He was always trying to spit that Gucci shit, and I don't speak Spanish.

COPS: Can we talk about "beauty hunger"?

JOSEPHINE: Not for nothing, honestly & truthfully, when it came to beauty, some of us had empty stomachs. My uncle Joe always told me you have to watch them when they lean to talk, watch to see if they wipe crumbs off your lip. I'm not a poet, mister, but I can see.

COPS: And what was it you saw that night?

JOSEPHINE: Love is where the paper unfolds unto itself. When I'm lying, my tongue seeks shelter, the horoscopes get the shit wrong, and I don't believe in emergency numbers. Might as well hang me on a wall and look at me all day. I pick up speed when I turn the corner.

THE POETRY COPS TALK WITH NENA, CACHITA, SHAMEKA, AND ROSIE

COPS: You girls were at the Sweet 16 when the Crazy Bunch crashed.

NENA: I don't know where you see a "girl" in this room, mister.

CACHITA: Right?

COPS: Pardon me.

CACHITA: The whole Block was at the Sweet 16.

NENA: That's where I met my husband.

SHAMEKA: You want to know about Petey, don't you?

COPS: Well, yes, Petey was absent from the party.

SHAMEKA: Did you ask the streets? The streets are always watching.

CACHITA: When you get born into this world, you have to figure out why you here quick.

COPS: But we want to know more about the bodies, the deaths, the effect it had on Skinicky. He was the poet in the crew.

CACHITA: On who?

NENA: The who?

COPS: Papo.

SHAMEKA: That nigga good. I heard he's living upstate. In the woods, and shit.

ROSIE: Whose body?

SHAMEKA: You can't have my body. My body, your body.

CACHITA: Everybody wants my body.

ROSIE: Like you, right, mister? You born to ask questions.

SHAMEKA: And I wasn't born to answer them. What bodies you talking about, mister?

Close to the River

The Block was on easy listening by the time we crossed
    the Bridge.

One could say that the moon over Lexington was sartorial. You
    could break the eerie down as fog without London; the
    light posts were holding a note, and no one was sitting
    on the abandoned folding chair that belonged to the
    community center.

There's always a cat, but now there's three and you swear
    that there's someone on the rooftop making faces at
    the stars.

When you get back to the Block in the wee hours, you become
    guru & guide, you acquire skills in asking the right
    questions, you know where the '98 Seville hood is headed,
    where a sign is missing, how close you were to the Spot by
    the small montage of red dots on a taxi's tail.

You ponder the lull after the cheese lines have closed, and
    you're left to wonder how your best customer finally
    hit bottom.

A pickup game picks up trash talk by the good net. Crickets &
    distant sirens decide to collaborate in this hour.

A leaf storm collages a backboard.

You didn't dare question the empty shopping cart near the
    garbage can.

A shade swallows half the street, and the need to get paid takes
    over the whole body.

It was no surprise that we lived close to the river; it was easy to
    make bastards of our era.

On the cool side of Gaddafi's, where the *viejos* sipped their
    Johnnie Walker nips with milk chasers, gibbous strands
    escaped through a missing doorknob, and two milk crates
    were left bottom-side-up like hints ready to be clocked.

The blood always draws a map. The longitude swirls under the
    icebox. The latitude draws a straight line, and you still
    can't find your way.

Angel was the first to see the yellow tape. He found Nestor in
    a pile of what we swore to forget: left eye by his foot, bile
    the shade of old butter, peppermint juice running down his
    cheeks, a crust commandeering his eyelids & cockroaches
    yelling obscenities from his diarrhea.

I've known rivers outlining this gangster right to the gutter.

A siren splotches the street new by the second. The nooks in the
    sewer lids mimic a petri dish, & you could dial the hotline
    behind the peeled billboard.

Cover him. Fucking cover him, Angel yells from behind the
    yellow tape.

None of us wanted to exit this world without a sense of
    procession while the whole Block was watching; no matter
    how much we stole, no matter how much we owed.

Chino Chan started a fake fight, and drew Teddy-Up to us.

Angel took a running start and cleared the top of the tape. He
    dropped to his knees, shrouded Nestor's face with a red
    BVD, and cried so much he almost got arrested.

Who was there to see what became of us at the touch
    of blood?

How It Went Down

A man walks into Gaddafi's with a cactus on his head. This sounds like the beginning of a joke, but it's not. We called him Gaddafi, but his name was Domingo. We called him Gaddafi because he looked like Gaddafi. The cactus wanted three-for-ten. When you take shorts, you can only take as much as been took, but when you're taken, then you need to start thinking about what they're calling *theirs* & what you're calling *yours*. The car that suddenly pulls up is more delivery than package. More end stop than ellipsis. The Dreads sit there & perch there & chill there & lamp there & chill there & rest there, still there, word, they don't move. Nestor let the Dreads know that nothing was happening, even though he just opened up. Petey says, *I heard those cactuses never die.* They say that getting shot is a scene study where all your reward circuits go blank. You only remember the blast, the smoke after the blast, the nanosecond after the smoke, and then you remember the cactus, untouched, sitting on the stoop, still, there.

Not for Nothing, Honestly & Truthfully

Like jewel thieves, we put everything to the light.
Whenever Brother Lo preambled stories with *Not
for nothing, honestly & truthfully*, we knew he was
lying his way into history. Stories started their
premises on the stoop, broke arcs by the time
they reached the uptown express, and the real
was played & buried by the time it got directions.
He said, *It was like Petey had a lit birthday candle
sticking out his right ass cheek. The negus ran all
the way to North General.* Shameka said she saw
a wisp of smoke flirting with the heat, a graph of
blood followed west all the way to triage. She
started telling stories, and hasn't stopped since.
Petey jetted to the hospital with a slug below
his heart, a skin shot near his calf, a cap in his
ass, and *don't call it symbolic,* Brother Lo told
Skinicky. *A man gots to know his wrong even
when he's turning blue. You just can't call the
wrong witch.* Before Petey went black, he saw
Nestor's mother cry into a blanket, a calendar
with a photo of the White Mountains, a body
bent in a wheelchair, a waterfall, and an empty
plastic cup. And then, the next thing you know,
you prayed hard, but you never made promises.

When Teddy-Up Rolls

We were already trapped in fire & abandonment, allies & alliances, villains & vandals, riding the twin engines of vigil & violence; we defended the Constitution better than the Constitution defended the Constitution.

When Teddy-Up rolled they rolled with new-world thirst.

Like a good mix, they shook the Block up & down until all the fried snitches fell out.

Embroidered the projects with scare tactics, kept their narratives consistent, checked their sources between punk & pussy, gossip & gore, and paid you to keep score.

Your thirst for aesthetics & answers begins here with a simple phrase.

Put your hands in the air like you just don't dare. Fingers together, belowdecks together. Click, now spread. Let me see the light come through.

Put your hands in the air like you just don't care. Who will scrub the floor with your breath plea, who will post it live, who will say, *That's not me.*

Everything you believed about being good starts to make a list in your head, and don't even start with your worldview.

Put your hands in the air like it just ain't fair, and now it's time for question & answer:

That was your who?
By show of hands, your relationship to freedom is what?
You said that was your boo?
Check out my melody &
Keep them up until I say different.

And the correct answer for a free—

*O me me me me me
me me me me me me.*

No ID

Always put a badge number to memory.

Teddy-Up's neck blushed a Christmas red.

Teddy-Up gripped his nightstick &
his knuckles ran Christmas white.

Angel was thinking, *Run.*
Angel was thinking, *That's my heart right there.*
Angel was thinking, *Mighty Whitey don't play fair.*
Angel was thinking, *Big beat big beat big beat.*
Angel was thinking, *Fuck the police.*
Angel was thinking, *I ain't running nowhere.*

I need to see ID before I let you go, said Teddy-Up.

Angel closed his eyes and said,

I'm nobody.
I don't have an ID.
I don't exist.
I was just walking to the store.
I'm not trying to resist.
I don't mess with that no more.

This is when you add a knuckle game to the triple feature.

Teddy-Up bounces Angel off an old movie poster.
The star's front tooth is blacked out.
A dialogue bubble reads, *I'm better off dead.*

Horns were scratched onto Cinderella's
pigtails, purple moons colored her eyes.

Angel looked like a Taíno Valentino with
a Young Lord Afro, six-packed to his core,
a study of hearts that never pumped Kool-Aid.

Not for nothing, honestly & truthfully,
you would later say,

That shit was like a movie.

YOU LOSE SOMETHING EVERY DAY

You Lose Something Every Day

It was Dre who once said,
You lose something every day

Your mind on the way to the store
The floor on the way to your mind
Your mind on your way to the clinic
The clinic on the way to one more

The mad in the way of your kind
The lyrics to your favorite song
The cure on the way to the camp
The finish on your way to the line

Your nickel in the way of a dime
The short to your favorite long
The loss on the way to the find
The skin that was yours to bare

The crown that was yours to wear
The floor you were forced to clean
The game that was yours to fair
The face you were pushed to mean

It was Dre who once said,
You lose something every day

Revival

Another Saturday night revival down the Block, and a pulpit full
      of Born Agains two-step past the chicken slaughterhouse.

Full moon and we still couldn't see each other, still couldn't
      reach that upper air. In the same breath, we discovered that
      you can't be Jesus's son when you're in front of a gun.

Pamphlets & speakers circulated the word,
& saving us was never on the court's docket.

O crackling tombstones.

Devil, the Sister sang, *don't get dressed because you ain't invited.*

Dre spit to the tambourine:

I get baptized in the sunrise /
Got realized in the wise & whys.

The Reverend spit too:

Cleanse the street off you, son.
Stop your life lie.
Come and brave this damn nation.
Do or die, as you say.

Who was it on lookout that yelled from the rooftop,

      Dre, who you trying to be, bro?

How to describe that sound when the birds flutter like a deck
      of cards being shuffled? Where to find your uplift &
      hallelujah, hosanna & hero, *campana* & chorus?

Dre plopped to his knees and cried, *It wasn't me. It wasn't me. It*
      wasn't me.

A crown of circus tents, two-headed spotlights, steady go tell it
on a mountain, & still no Glory for the crew.

Surround systems & cement trucks parked by No Parking. Trust
& believe, there was enough mix to bury all of us.

Where Did We Find the Laughter?

How to measure the end of summer before policy & polls,
    before seen, saw & said something, before lie, law &
    lost something.

All the lyrical legislators slipped a smart
bomb into our drinks; our cuts & tracks
were found facedown in a vault filled to
the brim with standing-room-only facts.

Give us a bag of wet, mark us in a soft spotlight, provide a laugh
    track, and there still wouldn't be anything funny, so let's
    frame Saturday night with Dre once again.

Syrup on his whiting Dre
Honey on his tuna Dre
Black Ethiopian Jew Dre
DeWitt Clinton High School Dre
Angel-dusted, naked, dick swinging in defiance of a heat
    wave Dre
Augusta Savage bronze in a 100-yard dash down Lexington
    Avenue, spirit chasing like whoa, & from our beach chairs
    all we could do was point and say, *Oh shit, that's Dre.*

There were some of us sitting there who could tell when Dre was
    punched or slapped by the way the walls in our building
    Richter-scaled.

Who was it that saw him jackknife out the sixth-floor window?
    His white yarmulke gyrated like a dizzy UFO, and what
    remained of Dre but his anchor & fishnet chain dangling
    off the sliding board?

You once asked, *Yo, where do we come from? Like, really come
    from? Like, from where? Like, where does that bomb-
    diggy-dang need to sing our corners come from?*

Brother Lo used to say, *It's been scientifically proven that a negus can put the universe in a headlock.*

Check the way we laugh now when we think of Dre, as if to say,

Shit ain't funny, man.

THE POETRY COPS

COPS: *It wasn't me.* What was Dre referring to?

PAPO: Dre smoked a bag that was too wet. I told you already, I don't know who bodied Nestor, and it wasn't Dre, if that's what you're getting at.

COPS: A wet bag?

PAPO: Purple Rain. Crazy Eddie. Zoo Bang.

COPS: Did someone throw him off the rooftop?

PAPO: It would've been better that way, but Dre threw Dre off the rooftop.

COPS: But how to know if no one saw?

PAPO: The whole Block saw.

COPS: What else did you see?

PAPO: I already told you what I didn't see.

COPS: Nestor, Petey on Friday. Dre on Saturday. That's a lot of bodies.

PAPO: That was a jackpot, a weekend trifecta, a straight number hit.

COPS: Did Dre ever say anything about suicide?

PAPO: Nigga couldn't kill himself right, man.

Freshly Dipped

That night Dre visits in a dream.

Freshly dipped,
24-karat name bracelet &
a halo on his pinky.

We had been sworn to silence and Rakim spoke for the crew
when he said, *I ain't no joke.*

C'mon, Dre says, *it's about to rain that Puerto Rico rain.*

Nestor's there too. He says, *This block is my island.* Then he did
his best Slick Rick imitation and sang, *"All alone, no one to
be with."*

Petey calculates bundle percentages near a bread loaf.

The icebox in front of Gaddafi's whirls into a tombstone, and
you hear a voice that you heard before, a voice that says,
Ain't nothing happening.

Skin & bone flip to dust & ash.

Your vapor oozes out of the icebox with a report from St.
Raymond's Cemetery: Charlie from the group home is
still pitching chronic, T-Lai-Rock has designs on making a
comeback to the Land of the Living, and Dwight said he
got one more nut in him.

Héctor Lavoe & Billie Holiday sing a duet.

Ask the dead, they know life, says Brother Lo.

And before Dre leaps into the icebox, he says, *Yo, you know
how they say that the soul leaves the body when you die?
Wait till you see what part of the body it exits from, bro.*

And, boom, he was ghost.

Each One Teach One

&

what dribbled out when the Block
coughed at the end of the night?

A Superman action figure
Purple 5 food stamps
Golden Glove wannabes
Mighty Mouse cheese lines
A Dapper Dan Gucci watch
A ticket to the Celebrity Club
A bevy of Yamahas throttling down 7th
A dope MC at the Rooftop
A Woo Hah trope & a Skate Key stopper
Claw's cankered forearm
Mikey's pigeon coup
Abuelita's chicken soup
The parade float
The honey on the float
The honey right off the boat
Straight sentences
No pleas
A rat cheesin' in the garbage
A sunset surfing the Harlem Line
Tenant patrol flyers
A silent accomplice
A firefly in the jar
A pair of faded jeans
A portrait in lattice
Co-opted ciphers
An old *Life* magazine
A preacher's splintered head
Two rusty badges

A cluster of pill bottles
A combination lock
A corroded Sugar Hill LP
A drive-by greeting card
A message with gears
A primal scream
A gangster's last wish,
Unpaid bills &
A beatbox—

Like Each One Teach One Ethiop used to say,

Those ain't bodies washing up on the street. Those are receipts.

FORGET WHAT YOU SAW

Forget What You Saw

I.

You want to see.

    You're in the whip, looking.

        You want to be seen as you see.

You want to be seen,

    and having been seen,

        never seen again.

There's hurt in your eye; it's been there since

    the Dutch set up shop.

You ain't running from nothing,

    but you ain't chasing nothing either.

Looking. As in,

    the best way to watch was the

        other way.

To see before they could say, *I saw*.

You lean to the side & recline, only to see

    Who else is hurting.

This is how you decide to gaze these days.

II.

Who

This, That & the Third,

      always looking for something.

Light most definitely, black. Bite the

      sky off it, man.

Bring some, they said,

         you talkin' so much.

The shook ones always live in

           running starts.

What Block was that again?

      Who was that you said again?

         Who you again?

Those tales

      lie best on nights like these—

Who tried to at least.

Fly, shoot—

      Please, shhhhh.

III.

Yours go bling Black,

      Black uh Black uh brain

          split &

              spilling,

                    spilling,

              & spilling.

Your oral history, a constant balm

      for the first walk-in & last testament.

Hunger, all teeth,

      no showtime to eat,

          apart from money

what did we spend &

      send all the green back.

The starting line ends here,

      in the Land of Ballers &

Shot Callers, the Land of

      Cuban links & *chocofan.*

Sink as far bottom as you can, you decide.

But why always why always always

       why

          always everything everything got to be

             about love, just wondering god—

it's true, you could be a lot of things given

       everything that's out

              there.

IV.

Forget what you saw

       people Who

Know this for sure

       are very suspicious

          of this Nothing.

This is a stickup.

       Don't make it a

          Bonnie.

Blood is always looking for

       a subject, a little something

about the Beginning before

        it starts, the attempts

             to find

yourself at off-peak hours; no

        images would be perfect for

this chill in the cut. Swear to God &

             Kaboom—

Bodies fall faster than

        stock prices, seen more

            than the time it takes

        to forget.

The thing is, though, not to

        stay behind &

            take the Life

                that was taken

        from you.

FORGET WHAT YOU HEARD

THE POETRY COPS

PAPO: You have to forget what you heard, even if you were out there when it happened.

COPS: But how to stay true to what you see?

PAPO: I wrote what I saw in the face of what I remember.

COPS: Well, who is the *you*?

PAPO: The *you* is you. Us, we, all of them, and the others. That's you.

COPS: Let's continue.

PAPO: That's all. I'm just trying to build.

COPS: Let's talk about Voice.

PAPO: Okay. Voice. On any Saturday night you could find yourself running against your voice. The voice that yells Five-O Teddy-Up is about to jump. That voice that suggests you don't go down a certain block, that you stay away from that blond streak, that you go home early, that at any moment your screams can go dry.

COPS: What happens when Voice comes to stay?

PAPO: Like Baraka used to say, *I can see something in the way of ourselves.*

COPS: That sounds like Brother Lo.

PAPO: You don't know patience until you stand on the corner when shit is slow. Brother Lo was on some planet rock shit. He made sure that we enlisted in the fight for freedom—not now, but right now.

Forget What You Heard

Heard you tried to win her back
Heard the new stamp was wack

Heard you was mad at your girl
Heard you was mad at the world

Heard your girl was fucking your boy
Heard your girl was fucking your toy

Heard you were smoking woos again
Heard you were breaking rules again

Heard you stopped going to the club
Heard you found where lies the rub

Heard there was poison in your cake
Heard there was honor at high stake

Heard the screw was trapped in a lug
Heard the crew was set up with a bug

Heard you never gave up the sugar
Heard you still picking your boogers

Heard the kings were high in the rubble
Heard the beginning was always trouble

Brother Lo on the Prison Industrial Complex

Brother Lo was a story master, a library without a card, a *cuento*
    king who could drop fables about the Young Lords, the
    spiritual value of Japanese swords, the degree of separation
    between concrete & rain, ice cream & pain.

He once said, *One hand can't wash the other if you're busy
    counting with your fingers.*

He also said, *The law is one top spin after another and bankrolls
    beget death tolls.*

This was before the two baddest buildings in the city were
    knocked out with a fuel-injected Guernica, before the
    urban planners had a jones for busting libraries.

The so-called bar starts early, says Brother Lo.

Starts with a permission slip for a class trip to the local precinct.
Starts with *If you see something, you better not say shit.*
Your teacher will urge you to get excited.
Free mug shots if you behave.
You're going to get arrested like it was for real:
cheese sandwiches, sour milk, dented oranges
& a hint of ammonia in your cough.

There will even be a contest to see how long you can stay
    handcuffed to a classmate before you decide to throw him
    under the bus.

Before you leave the school, your teacher will ask you to line up
    for a head count.

It should be fun, your teacher will say.

Trip day comes and you see your first chain gang, a head speed-
    bumped into a desktop, a door creaking to a close on a
    confession.

The bus ride home will be less park than amusement.
The sirens will sound petrified, but happy.
Your mother doesn't believe in conspiracies, so she's good
    with it.
Your father was a revolutionary before he sold the revolution for
    two bundles & a quarter water.

When it's time to show & tell, the only thing you can remember
    is standing on line, waiting for copies of your free mug
    shots, and right before you left the precinct, you heard the
    desk sergeant taking odds that half the class will come back
    arrested for real.

The Whole World on a Subway

According to Brother Lo, you will go to court and find the whole world on the subway.

Coffee cup lids will spit impatient steams and a blind man with two good legs will say, *This don't look like what it seems.*

You will see a brother named Lucky, and as soon as he sees you he will start talking open cases, rehab, programs, offers, pleas & deals.

You will look for something that can hold the weight, and come upon a poem, a subway poem, a poem in transit, a poem about planks & experience—twice.

By the time you reach 96th Street, you'll detect a heartbroken voice yell, *Damn, why don't you fucking say excuse me!*

A brother named Jose (it will say *Jose* on his Lenox Hill Hospital Dickie) will tap out a happy hour blues with his rolled-up *Daily News*. You will learn the beat by heart and scat it from Reception to Reentry.

At 59th Street, a walking confectionary will almost go to hell with a sweet tooth for stepping on Lucky's high-top shell tops, and Lucky will have just finished saying that he's been looking for an excuse to lose it.

Instead, he will have a grill contest with a gray pinstripe, and Lucky, with his steel-toe eyes, will win all the way to Grand Central.

A kind soul will throw two nickels at the Section Eight Gospel Trio because it was still the city of trains that promised good skin & quick memory.

Right after you process the static of the conductor's
     announcement, the quietest woman in the subway car,
     rocking a natural bun—no balm, no blush—will stand up,
     point to Lucky & give him specific directions to Heaven
     with a list of who's going & who's staying.

The train will pull into Brooklyn Bridge station, and Lucky will
     say, *Fuck it, if the judge offers me a two-to-four, I'm gonna
     take it.*

Bullshit Walks

Bullshit steps
To a global beat.

Buffs a shine for
His smile from

A green mile
Away &

Daps you a
Strong pound.

Says we boys,
Bro, we boys.

Styles & profiles
Two on the

Hip & Raps
Along with

Boom & Parties
& Bullshit.

Yawns in between
Fibs to pregnant

Women, & flips
On demand.

There should be
A special car on

The 2 train
Just for Bull-

Shitters laughing
The night away &

Choking on a snack
Box with extra lies.

Drug War Confidential

Let me just say, right now, that we can't stop won't stop. We're
    in the trillions and still on the come up. What took the
    Bunch so long? Your number was called last week. Late
    then, later now.

Well, why are we here?

Tell us, what's going on up there? We want to know.

You mean down there.

No, right here.

False claims, fake news, old blues, blood & feathers, gold &
    water, bad weather, black bodies, brown detentions, low
    retentions, you know, same ole same ole.

Well, shit, let's celebrate.

But we're supposed to be free now, man.

Y'all were free then.

We're just learning how to love, man. Leave us be.

Nah, that's a game for the played, my young brothers.

This can't be the end. Where all my people? Where's my Block?

Don't waste our morning, man. It's time to go.

Why those Burners all up in my face like that, all mean?

Well, how many ways did you choose to be alive? Revolution,
    say amen. Every fight should request a repeat. We ask, you
    answer. That's the way it is down here.

You mean right here.

Oh, you must think we're joking.

Then why you smiling? What's so funny, man?

And here we were, right in the middle of building a pill free of
time. Who are all these women wearing white and smoking
cigars? Why are they looking at the sun, why are they
pointing three fingers at us?

All is fair in love and drug wars, homie. You ain't the only one
taking pictures.

A SPOT WHERE YOU CAN KISS THE DEAD

■

Breaking Night

In that year of a shot to the head where were you the first time
    you broke night?

When you break night, you learn that one puff, under the right
    circumstance, can give you the right perspective.

You learn to pick up stories that fall & slip on the right side of
    knowing.

What is it, a blizzard? That was a summer riff, should you be
    confronted with the choice of fight or fun.

The call from the rooftop used to be *boombellumboom,*
    and the sky would go back to its specific blue places.

The Block wakes to sun & skeleton. You could talk to God for
    free, water bread swan-dived off groggy trucks, & your
    soul begged for the breakfast special.

Bodega gates slammed open like start guns, and that's when you
    tried to predict the future.

A formal wind is all we needed to keep cool.

On that Sunday sunrise, we laughed because we saw the light
    for the first time; the light that breaks bread & the light the
    dead sing when it's time for that last surge.

The rock doves atop the light posts coo-cooed our direction
    home: always north, always uptown.

There we were, still wearing our hallway hickeys, and someone
    had to pay for the Buddha Thai, the brown suede Ballys &
    the party socks.

Fuck all those bubble-gum-chewing, the-personal-ain't-political
    mornings—it was time to swim.

One by one, we picked each other up until there was enough
    crew to stock a lineup.

The park was already fired up with cauldrons of *gandules* &
    asopao, all kinds of fricassee, & long-grain *Canilla* served
    with the story of an uprising.

Foils & forks, napkins & wipes, gizzards & tripe, the concept of
    an extended noon, & learning how to feed someone with a
    long spoon.

In the *madrugada* we found a Big Beat, a homeostatic way of
    hanging out, spin styles & salvation, *word to my mother*
    became our true signature.

The math was easy that morning. We wanted to open spots
    where we could feel syncretic.

Language, the Old-Schoolers used to say, was a lemon running
    up the stairs, a piano plink, an uppercut & right cross.

Ain't you somethin', you the same one, we'd like to say.

Metro-North rattles, more battles to be won, & part of the game
    was to be torn out of one's frame.

Cherry blossoms caked on Mount Morris octagons, and the
    M116 rumbled a tune of transfers straight out the depot.

Get the sun in your life, son.
You're my sun because you shine,
not because you're mine, son.

We ran over the mountain, walked the line on a dead steam
    pipe like a Wallenda, check it—that's where all the favors
    go down.

The ghost of nasty Rucker Park crossovers. A highlight reel of
     sucker turnovers.

Doing it in the dark
Doing it in the dark
Oh yeah

We could've been six feet under for all we knew, so we hopped
     the public pool gates, & swam 400-hundred-meter relays
     in our soaked boxers.

Created teams & heats, bets for next,
& banged out beats waiting for our legs.

Homeroom & homecomings, study hall & Scholastic had
     lost their appeal. Being cool, being real, crashing hooky
     sets, being rookie'd into gang divisions, the smell of sex
     & grown-up talk, that's what we knew of freedom. No
     regulations, no rules made to fit the latest trend, no rules to
     regulate the fool in us. That morning, all we wanted to find
     was a smile at the bottom of the world.

On Sundays

On Sundays we composed our own music.

Tapped a nickel against a mailbox,
pounded the wall with the heel of our
palms, and sought a demo-type sound.

Sundays were the sound of a tobacco patch crashing on the tip
of a boot.
The nimbus of gospel & game rejoicing at the feet of laughter
& loot.

Saint Martin held us down in word if not in deed.
Santa Barbara held us down in word if not in need.
San Lazaro held us down in pocket if not in feed.

On Sundays, number slips trickled from Maxi's
sleeves, & dream books slept on discount racks.

Sundays were for your best clothes, which meant that every day
was Sunday.

Two birds sat on a crucifix, and grandma's church
hat was damn near auctioned at the Player's Ball.

Sundays were for sonnets & aunties, bonnets & Bibles, a
mourning dove nesting near your window guard, a rumor
upgraded to libel, making babies to a faint chirp & being
late to your Confirmation.

Everything damn near legal was damn near closed on Sunday.

On Sundays, we had to give up a piece of our burning.

Trago*

Some of us stopped going to wakes since *difunto* Orlando. Chuna stays outside because he has nightmares whenever he stands near a casket. Loco Tommy cracks the first pint of dark rum and Phat Phil pulls out a Polaroid. You remember when the flick was taken at the Block party because Skinicky spent a grip trying to win a teddy bear for Josephine.

It was the day Dre, Nestor, Los, Sinbad, and Bam Bam decided to split everything five ways. Dre was looking at the camera like a coyote who wants you to think he's smiling. His Burner was aimed at the lens; it was the last group shot of a death squad that had long since stopped talking about the latest dances.

When all the plastic cups are filled, Loco Tommy gives Papá Dios a quick shout and says, *Look out for Nestor, man. We're sending him correct. He got a gold rope wrapped around his prayer hands and he ain't wearing boots, so he should be okay to get in.*

We all take a *trago* at the same time and then someone starts talking about Nestor and monsters.

Loco Tommy squashes it. *If anyone asks*, he says, *it was cancer. Everything is cancer.*

*From *Smoking Lovely* by Willie Perdomo. Used and adapted by permission of the author. He was cool with me using this poem.

THE POETRY COPS

COPS: Is it true that you had to bury Dre, Nestor, and Petey at the same time, on the same day?

PAPO: Just Nestor. Dre had his own mourning rites on St. Nicholas Avenue, and Petey was shipped to San Juan.

COPS: That much death can't be easy.

PAPO: It was like that with the Old-Schoolers. They didn't like to leave any traces, and they always made a point of keeping us in our places.

COPS: I imagine that much death makes it hard to measure what's fate and what's fair.

PAPO: You'd be surprised how quickly PTHD sets in.

COPS: You mean PTSD.

PAPO: No. I mean PTHD. Post-Traumatic Hood Disorder. You know, semiautomatic, up jump the boogie, olio, neighborhood registers, homegirls & hand grenades, the big smoke, the residue years, the sellout, wild hundreds, in visible movements, bright felons, roses in the mirror, bone shepherds, *mongo* affairs, all that shit sets in.

COPS: Can you tell us about this?

PAPO: Ortiz Funeral Home was a second home, a forever rest stop, a reverse dreaming, free rum, a workshop on *novenas*, a spot where you could kiss the dead. A place where you learned your friend's government name.

COPS: How to remember the dead?

PAPO: You have to open the door when they knock.

THE POETRY COPS

PAPO: German Shepherd Man used to intermission the Block every Sunday night. Black bucket hat, stars & rhinestone, all that. I remember. We were at that age where we still couldn't play the corner. I was about to shoot for my Killer Diller and Edgar said, "There he goes, there he goes, there goes German Shepherd Man." (Matter of fact, it was Edgar that gave him his name.) That night, summer was fat. Heat like a vat of hot showers, and closer to Park Avenue, German Shepherd Man's silhouette glimmered all the way to Mount Morris. I just remember the dogs' eyes were different shades of steel & cement. When they got below the el, the dogs stood at attention, three on his left, three on his right, and German Shepherd Man commanded them in beats & sharp breaths. *Who. What. Ho. Hey. Go. Shoot. Up. Hup.* Shameka had just arrived from Savannah—she was scared of dogs, so she watched from a fire escape. The dogs lined up in front of the picnic tables by the community garden. German Shepherd Man said, *Who,* and the dogs jumped up on the table, turned around, faced German Shepherd Man, and decorated the Block like a museum wing of statues. Then, German Shepherd Man talked in a whisper. And the dogs did an about-face, jumped off the table, three veered to his right, three to his left, and they walked west, back into the mist, and for a blip the Block was a silent film, but you could hear sweat drops rippling down your still-hairless underarms, a hunger knot curling in your stomach, a squad of flies feasting on a dirty diaper, & a dead body wrapped in a linoleum rug.

Killer Diller

Used to be
The end-

Game for
Skelsies.

Now, you jet
Down the

B-stair &
Hope you

Come out
Free.

It might be
True that the

Pursuit of
Liberty &

Happiness
Likes to go

Solo, but
Like we

Used to say
Over & over

Again:

Ain't no
Fun

If I can't get
None.

To Be Down

Who among us believed in the great scheme of life and still had
    enough stage presence to carry the night?

To be down, you had to start blindfolded at the top.
To be down by law, you die for one or you die for all.

One building, twelve stories of surprise confrontation, a portrait
    in mean, take as many steps to the end as needed.

Jet down the stairs all the way to the lobby.
Every odd-numbered floor was a place to breathe right quick.
No more than two people on any even floor could attack.
A death blow might jump out of every door;
if that was your hobby for real, you were good.

No fire extinguishers, no belts, no sticks, no
tricks, no rallies against your inborn dignity.

If you reached the stoop standing up, you were down.

You could cry, but you had to cry standing up.

And by no means would you allow yourself to become a cliché:
    broke at the end.

There's a golden mean that loves with a weak hand; it's part of
    our disembodied shade, and studies your face when you
    land on the come up.

Some might call it a thirst for manhood.

Quick to reach, quick to teach.

When you only have one chance,
it's never been about being fair.

What did it mean to be
yourself, to practice
staying alive, to cry
for those of us who
couldn't hit back?

Bust This, Run That

To break it down
You would say

Bust This.
To take without

Permission you
Would say

Run That.

To tell no lies you
Would say, *That's*

My word to
Everything I love.

To make a law
Unwritten,

You might get
Asked for your

Sneaker size,
A steady Vic

In his eyes, &
You would have

No choice but
To reply,

Your size.

They Won't Find Us in Books

And after we officially gained entry into the Brotherhood of
   Bad Motherfuckers, what could our mothers do but lose
   sleep, wake into prayer, prepare herbs & apples, cursive the
   names of our enemies on loose-leaf & let their names dust
   in the sunlight.

Now everything is clean, rezoned & paved, tenements
   abandoned like wack parties, what is left for us to do but
   summon bullies from their graves & liberate ourselves
   from influence.

Gone are the old spots near the takeout, old flames where we
   used to make out, the spots where the light used to fade
   out, and the letters we wrote from burning buildings.

Our shoulders were made of stone, our evil was translucent.
   Turn us into mortals, so we can cry without judgment,
   surrender our cool, and watch us morph into men.

Let it be known that we chased Killer Dillers before the cans got
   kicked for good.

We were made from repeating blocks.

Holler if you hear us.

There was never a *once upon a time* because all it takes is one
   person to get away with it, to get away & get over, to get
   some & get up, here we go, c'mon, here we go.

You our history, you said.

If being free means burning a few things, then play that number
   for us straight.

The corner was between us & the world, and sometimes you just
   needed to be okay with not telling.

If anyone asks you about your destiny, don't explain.

Maybe this is the story we need to turn ourselves into music,
     bass & bully, a string pulling at both ends.

They won't find us in books, you used to say.

Everybody say, *Yeah, and you don't stop.*

We practiced our lives in lobbies & layaway, ganders & goofs,
     boosting lines from the radio, breaking dynamite styles.
     We were god bodies, we had God in our bodies.

That's what Brother Lo used to say, he used to say,

A man can stand on the corner long enough to
see a dream etched on a Herb's forehead; to see
desperation exit from a subway station; to see
a tragic hero come back to reclaim his
     city,

so we downloaded his bars & gems, and, no doubt, when it was
     time to tell our story, out would come fire & spit.

Ghost Face

The ghost face grills a display of beans & detergent, picks his Afro like a cowboy in a saloon, and reflects on a memory of beatdowns & bruises, super friends & losers. No use in total recall. Remember that night when the muse decided to use the Block and left before the party started jumping? You want to say, *I know that walk,* but it's not what you thought because it's never what you think. And it's rare that you can get both at the same time. You listen for that volley of rubble king chants from rooftop to rooftop. On the real, coming back is a choice. All the cuchifrito joints are shut down, and the number hall now sells two-for-one pizza slices. Where's the crew? And someone yells from down the Block, *Comemierda, ven acá.* And what if you faded into the blackness of black, who would be there to say *Try me.* You definitely know the answer, but you can't be the first to say you saw something, otherwise you'll be the first to get asked.

THE POETRY COPS

COPS: Okay, we're going to ask you again.

PAPO: Ask me again.

COPS: Most of what you told us—

PAPO: When you're Poeting, and the feel is real, then you might as well cut the deck and deal. I'm not fronting on you right now. I'm really not. I'm just saying I found my bid to sing early; and when I found it, Judgment Day, which once ran local, announced that it was going express.

COPS: But the Readers might say—

PAPO: Ask Phat Phil, Baby Los, any of them brothers that are still around. When the bodies & blood began to add up, we were there to do the math.

COPS: Then it was your life as you saw it.

PAPO: Well, one could say it was as if my life saw me seeing my life and said, *Yo, Skinicky, when you gonna tell that story about the crew?* You ever break night with a brick?

COPS: Like a bad shot?

PAPO: For the record, it's fucked up how they banned those drums in Mount Morris Park. And, now, I go uptown and try to find friends in the faces of strangers. How to arrange yourself so that the ending is right?

COPS: Who was it that said death is the mother of beauty?

PAPO: I think it was Brother Lo.

COPS: No, it was—

PAPO: What I can tell you is that Shit & Fucked Up speak Spanish too. The image has a way of making you take a stand. So, if beauty is death's daughter, then where is that nigga's father?

SHOUT-OUTS & BIG UPS

A Gathering of the Tribes, The Yale Review, Poetry, Green Mountains Review, 2 Bridges Review, What Saves Us: Poems of Empathy and Outrage in the Age of Trump, The Common, Free Verse, Sun's Skeleton: Thanks for placing earlier versions of these poem stories in your journals and anthologies.

Vermont Studio Center, Phillips Exeter Academy, Cave Canem, East Harlem Tutorial Program, Lucas Artists Residency Program at Montalvo Arts Center, CantoMundo, Hurston/Wright Foundation, VONA/Voices of Our Nations Arts Foundation, City College of New York, Urban Word NYC, *The Poetry Gods*, Poets House, Bronx Museum of the Arts, Camaradas El Barrio, Los Gallos Social Club, the Titere Poets, *Cooley High*, and #PoetsforPuertoRico.

Leslie Shipman, Paul Slovak, Allie Merola, and Maria Massie: The Dream Keeper Crew.

Raymond R. Patterson, wish you were here. RIP. Like you said in '93, *a tale of the tribe*. East Harlem, stand up.

Ed Randolph, the Mad Poet of Harlem. I salute you.

Poet Homies: Patrick Rosal, Cynthia Dewi Oka, Sevé Torres, Tameka Cage Conley, Tyehimba Jess, David Tomas Martinez, Major Jackson, Didi Jackson, Fernando Lorenzo, Mitch Jackson, Vincent Toro, John Murillo, Nicole Sealey, Reginald Dwayne Betts, Afaa Michael Weaver, Belinda Toomer, Michael Bennett, Marcus Jackson, Millie Gonzalez, Randall Horton, George Guida, Paul Flores, Mercy Carbonell, Joseph Rios, Javier Zamora,

Greg Pardlo, Jeffery Renard Allen, Mitchell S. Jackson, Matt Miller, Ralph Sneeden, Michael Cirelli, Todd Hearon, Sami Atif, Khadijah Atif, Cameron Brickhouse, Ana Portnoy Brimmer, Denice Frohman, Noel Quiñones, and Rocio Peña. 100 shouts for weighing this brick. 100 *gracias* for chopping it up. 100 big ups for pushing your own bricks.

Paul Beatty, Tracy Sherrod, Renaldo Davidson, Mike Tyler, DCP, and Marie D. Brown, for always showing up at the right time.

To my children: BJ, Neruda, and Carmen. I'm not playing. Y'all better call me when you get home.

To my wife, my goddess, my everything: Sandra Perdomo, who was there the night this book made an unannounced visit. *Te amo, amada mía.*

WILLIE PERDOMO is the author of *The Crazy Bunch*; *The Essential Hits of Shorty Bon Bon*, a finalist for the National Book Critics Circle Award; *Smoking Lovely*, winner of the PEN/Open Book Award; and *Where a Nickel Costs a Dime*, a finalist for the Poetry Society of America's Norma Farber First Book Award. His work has appeared in *The New York Times Magazine*, *The Norton Anthology of Latino Literature*, *Poetry*, and *African Voices*. He is currently a member of the VONA/Voices faculty, a Lucas Arts Literary Fellow, and he teaches at Phillips Exeter Academy.

JOHN ASHBERY
Selected Poems
Self-Portrait in a Convex
    Mirror

PAIGE ACKERSON-KIELY
Dolefully, A Rampart
    Stands

PAUL BEATTY
Joker, Joker, Deuce

JOSHUA BENNETT
The Sobbing School

TED BERRIGAN
The Sonnets

LAUREN BERRY
The Lifting Dress

PHILIP BOOTH
Lifelines: Selected Poems
    1950–1999

JULIANNE BUCHSBAUM
The Apothecary's Heir

JIM CARROLL
Fear of Dreaming:
    The Selected Poems
Living at the Movies
Void of Course

ALISON HAWTHORNE DEMING
Genius Loci
Rope
Stairway to Heaven

CARL DENNIS
Another Reason
Callings
New and Selected Poems
    1974–2004
Night School
Practical Gods
Ranking the Wishes
Unknown Friends

DIANE DI PRIMA
Loba

STUART DISCHELL
Dig Safe

STEPHEN DOBYNS
Velocities: New and
    Selected Poems:
    1966–1992

EDWARD DORN
Way More West

ROGER FANNING
The Middle Ages

ADAM FOULDS
The Broken Word

CARRIE FOUNTAIN
Burn Lake
Instant Winner

AMY GERSTLER
Crown of Weeds
Dearest Creature
Ghost Girl
Medicine
Nerve Storm
Scattered at Sea

EUGENE GLORIA
Drivers at the Short-
    Time Motel
Hoodlum Birds
My Favorite Warlord

DEBORA GREGER
By Herself
Desert Fathers, Uranium
    Daughters
God
In Darwin's Room
Men, Women, and Ghosts
Western Art

TERRANCE HAYES
American Sonnets for
    My Past and Future
    Assassin
Hip Logic
How to Be Drawn
Lighthead
Wind in a Box

NATHAN HOKS
The Narrow Circle

ROBERT HUNTER
Sentinel and Other
    Poems

MARY KARR
Viper Rum

JACK KEROUAC
Book of Blues
Book of Haikus
Book of Sketches

JOANNA KLINK
Circadian
Excerpts from a Secret
    Prophecy
Raptus

JOANNE KYGER
As Ever: Selected Poems

ANN LAUTERBACH
Hum
If in Time: Selected
    Poems, 1975–2000
On a Stair
Or to Begin Again
Spell
Under the Sign

CORINNE LEE
Plenty

PHILLIS LEVIN
May Day
Mercury
Mr. Memory & Other
    Poems

PATRICIA LOCKWOOD
Motherland Fatherland
    Homelandsexuals

WILLIAM LOGAN
Macbeth in Venice
Madame X
Rift of Light
Strange Flesh
The Whispering Gallery

J. MICHAEL MARTINEZ
Museum of the Americas

ADRIAN MATEJKA
The Big Smoke
Map to the Stars
Mixology

MICHAEL MCCLURE
Huge Dreams: San
    Francisco and Beat
    Poems

ROSE MCLARNEY
Its Day Being Gone

DAVID MELTZER
David's Copy: The
    Selected Poems of
    David Meltzer

ROBERT MORGAN
Dark Energy
Terroir

CAROL MUSKE-DUKES
Blue Rose
An Octave Above
    Thunder
Red Trousseau
Twin Cities

ALICE NOTLEY
Certain Magical Acts
Culture of One
The Descent of Alette
Disobedience
In the Pines
Mysteries of Small
    Houses

WILLIE PERDOMO
The Crazy Bunch
The Essential Hits of
    Shorty Bon Bon

LIA PURPURA
It Shouldn't Have Been
    Beautiful

LAWRENCE RAAB
The History of Forgetting
Visible Signs: New and
    Selected Poems

BARBARA RAS
The Last Skin
One Hidden Stuff

MICHAEL ROBBINS
Alien vs. Predator
The Second Sex

PATTIANN ROGERS
Generations
Holy Heathen Rhapsody
Quickening Fields
Wayfare

SAM SAX
Madness

ROBYN SCHIFF
A Woman of Property

WILLIAM STOBB
Absentia
Nervous Systems

TRYFON TOLIDES
An Almost Pure Empty
    Walking

SARAH VAP
Viability

ANNE WALDMAN
Gossamurmur
Kill or Cure
Manatee/Humanity
Structure of the World
    Compared to a Bubble
Trickster Feminism

JAMES WELCH
Riding the Earthboy 40

PHILIP WHALEN
Overtime: Selected
    Poems

ROBERT WRIGLEY
Anatomy of Melancholy
    and Other Poems
Beautiful Country
Box
Earthly Meditations:
    New and Selected
    Poems
Lives of the Animals
Reign of Snakes

MARK YAKICH
The Importance of
    Peeling Potatoes in
    Ukraine
Unrelated Individuals
    Forming a Group
    Waiting to Cross